Machine Learning

Step-by-Step Guide To Implement

Machine Learning Algorithms with Python

Author

Rudolph Russell

Table of Contents

CHAPTER 1

INTRODUCTION TO MACHINE LEARNING

Theory

If I ask you about "Machine learning," you'll probably imagine a robot or something like the Terminator. In reality t, machine learning is involved not only in robotics, but also in many other applications. You can also imagine something like a spam filter as being one of the first applications in machine learning, which helps improve the lives of millions of people. In this chapter, I'll introduce you what machine learning is, and how it works.

What is machine learning?

Machine learning is the practice of programming computers to learn from data. In the above example, the program will easily be able to determine if given are important or are "spam". In machine learning, data referred to as called training sets or examples.

Why machine learning?

Let's assume that you'd like to write the filter program without using machine learning methods. In this case, you would have to carry out the following steps:

· In the beginning, you'd take a look at what spam e-mails looks like. You might select them for the words or phrases they use, like "debit card," "free," and so on, and also from patterns that are used in the sender's name or in the body of the email

· Second, you'd write an algorithm to detect the patterns that you've seen, and then the software would flag emails as spam if a certain number of those patterns are detected.

· Finally, you'd test the program, and then redo the first two steps again until the results are good enough.

Because the program is not software, it contains a very long list of rules that are difficult to maintain. But if you developed the same software using ML, you'll be able to maintain it properly.

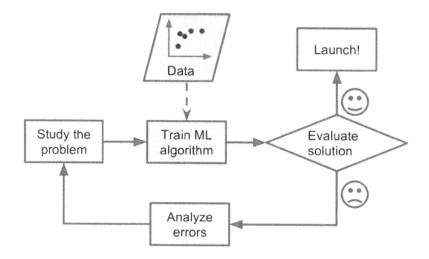

In addition, the email senders can change their e-mail templates so that a word like "4U" is now "for you," since their emails have been determined to be spam. The program using traditional techniques would need to be updated, which means that, if there were any other changes, you would l need to update your code again and again and again.

On the other hand, a program that uses ML techniques will automatically detect this change by users, and it starts to flag them without you manually telling it to.

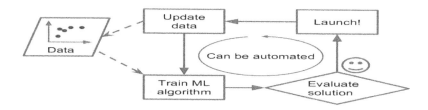

Also, we can use ,machine learning to solve problems that are very complex for non-machine learning software. For example, speech recognition: when you say "one" or "two", the program should be able to distinguish the difference. So, for this task, you'll need to develop an algorithm that measures sound.

In the end, machine learning will help us to learn, and machine-learning algorithms can help us see what we have learned.

When should you use machine learning?

• When you have a problem that requires many long lists of rules to find the solution. In this case, machine-learning techniques can simplify your code and improve performance.

• Very complex problems for which there is no solution with a traditional approach.

• Non- stable environments': machine-learning software can adapt to new data.

Types of Systems of Machine Learning

There are different types of machine-learning systems. We can divide them into categories, depending on whether

• They have been trained with humans or not

- Supervised
- Unsupervised
- Semi-supervised
- Reinforcement Learning
• If they can learn incrementally

• If they work simply by comparing new data points to find data points, or can detect new patterns in the data ,and then will build a model.

Supervised and unsupervised learning

We can classify machine learning systems according to the type and amount of human supervision during the training. You can find four major categories, as we explained before.

- Supervised learning
- Unsupervised learning
- Semi-supervised learning
- Reinforcement learning

Supervised Learning

In this type of machine-learning system, the data that you feed into the algorithm, with the desired solution, are referred to as "labels."

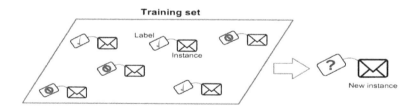

- Supervised learning groups together a tasks of classification. The above program is a good example of this because it's been trained with many emails at the same time as their class.

Another example is to predict a numeric value like the price of a flat, given a set of features (location, number of rooms, facilities) called predictors; this type of task is called regression.

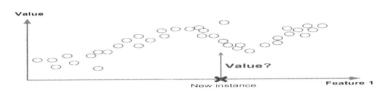

You should keep in mind that some regression algorithms can be used for classifications as well, and vice versa.

The most important supervised algorithms

- K-nears neighbors
- Linear regression
- Neural networks
- Support vector machines
- Logistic regression
- Decision trees and random forests

Unsupervised Learning

In this type of machine-learning system, you can guess that the data is unlabeled.

- **Clustering**: k-means, hierarchical cluster analysis
- **Association rule learning**: Eclat, apriori
- **Visualization and dimensionality reduction**: kernel PCA, t-distributed, PCA

As an example, suppose you've got many data on visitor Using of one of our algorithms for detecting groups with similar visitors. It may find that 65% of your visitors are males who love watching movies in the evening, while 30% watch plays in the evening; in this case, by using a clustering algorithm, it will divide every group into smaller sub-groups.

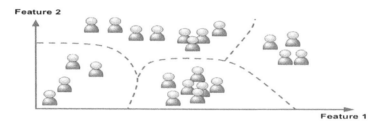

There are some very important algorithms, like visualization algorithms; these are unsupervised learning algorithms. You'll need to give them many data and unlabeled data as an input, and then you'll get 2D or 3D visualization as an output.

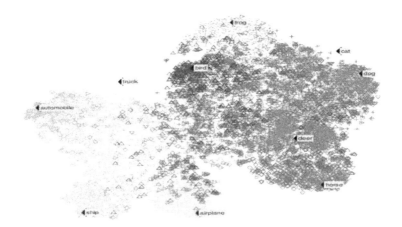

The goal here is to make the output as simple as possible without losing any of the information. To handle this problem. it will combine several related features into one feature: for example, it will cmbn a car's make with its model. This is called feature extraction.

Reinforcement Learning

Reinforcement learning is another type of machine-learning system. An agent "AI system" will observe the environment, perform given actions, and then receive t rewards in return. With this type, the agent must learn by itself. Ties called a policy.

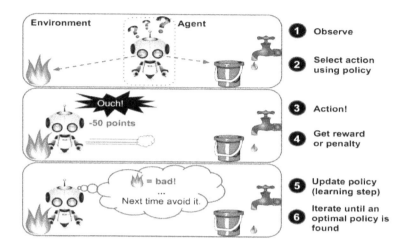

You can find this type of learning type in many robotics applications that learn how to walk

Batch Learning

In this kind of machine-learning systems, the system can't learn incrementally: the system must obtain all the needed data . That means it will require many resources and a huge amount of time, so it's always done offline. So, to work with this type of learning, the first thing to do is to train the system, and then launch it without any learning.

Online Learning

This kind of learning is the opposite of batch learning. I mean that, here, **the system can learn incrementally by providing the system with** all the available data as instances (groups or individually), and then the system can learn on the fly.

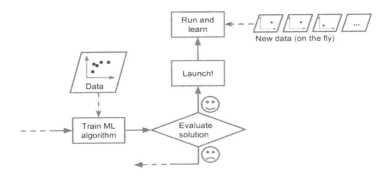

You can use this type of system for problems that require the continuous flow of data, which also needs to adapt quickly to any changes. Also, you can use this type of system to work with very large data sets,

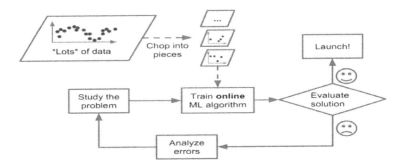

You should know how fast your system can adapt to any changes in the data's "learning rate." If the speed is high, means that the system will learn quite, quickly, but it also will forget old data quickly.

Instance based learning

This is the simplest type of learning that you should learn by heart. By using this type of learning in our email program, it will flag all of the emails that were flagged by users.

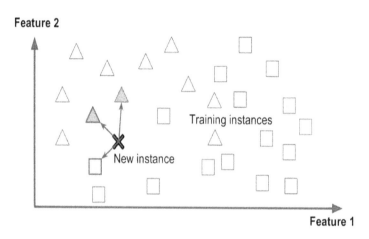

Model-based learning

There is another type of learning in which learning from examples allows construction to make predictions

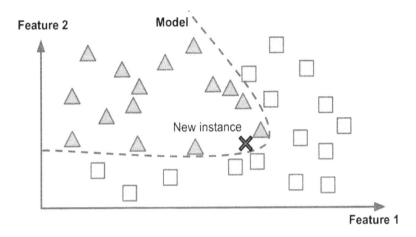

Bad and Insufficient Quantity of Training Data

Machine-learning systems are not like children, who can distinguish apples and oranges in all sorts of colors and shapes, but they require lot of data to work effectively, whether you're working with very simple programs and problems, or complex applications like image processing and speech recognition. Here is an example of the unreasonable effectiveness of data, showing the MS project, which includes simple data and the complex problem of NLP.

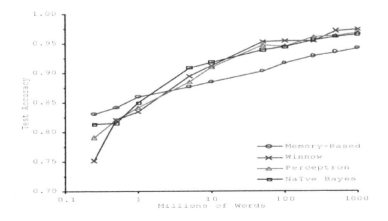

Poor-Quality Data

If you're working with training data that is full of errors and outliers, this will make it very hard for the system to detect patterns , so it won't work properly. So, if you want your program to work well, you must spend more time cleaning up your training data.

Irrelevant Features

The system will only be able to learn if the training data contains enough features and data that aren't too irrelevant. The most important part of any ML project is to develop good features "of feature engineering".

Feature Engineering

The process of feature engineering goes like this:

. **Selection of features:** selecting the most useful features.

. **Extraction of features:** combining existing features to provide more useful features.

. **Creation of new features**: creation of new features, based on data.

Testing

If you'd like to make sure that your model is working well and that model can generalize with new cases, you can try out new cases with it by putting the model in the environment and then monitoring how it will perform. This is a good method, but if your model is inadequate, the user will complain.

You should divide your data into two sets, one set for training and the second one for testing, so that you can train your model using the first one and test it using the second. The generalization error is the rate of error by evaluation of your model on the test set. The value you get will tell you if your model is good enough, and if it will work properly.

If the error rate is low, the model is good and will perform properly. In contrast, if your rate is high, this means your model will perform badly and not work properly. My advice to you is to use 80% of the data for training and 20% for testing purposes, so that it's very simple to test or evaluate a model.

Overfitting the Data

If you're in a foreign country and someone steals something of yours, you might say that everyone is a thief. This is an overgeneralization, and, in machine learning, is called "overfitting". This means that machines do the same thing: they can perform well when they're working with the training data, but they can't generalize them properly. For example, in the following figure you'll find a high degree of life satisfaction model that overfits the data, but it works well with the training data.

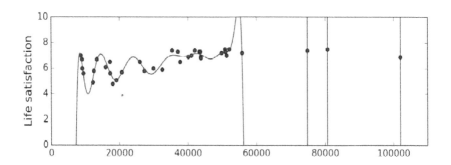

When does this occur?

Overfitting occurs when the model is very complex for the amount of training data given.

Solutions

To solve the overfitting problem, you should do the following:

- Gather more data for "training data"
- Reduce the noise level
- Select one with fewer parameters

Underfitting the Data

From its name, underfitting is the opposite of overfitting, and you'll encounter this when the model is very simple to learn. For example, using the example of quality of life, real life is more complex than your model, so the predictions won't yield the same, even in the training examples.

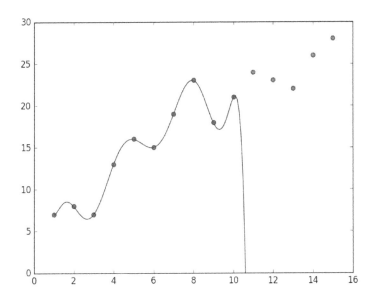

Solutions

To fix this problem:

- Select the most powerful model, which has many parameters.
- Feed the best features into your algorithm. Here, I'm referring to feature engineering.
- Reduce the constraints on your model.

EXERCISES

In this chapter, we have covered many concepts of machine learning. The following chapters will be very practical, and you'll write code, but you should answer the following questions just to make sure you're on the right track.

1. Define machine learning

2. Describe the four types of machine-learning systems.

3. What is the difference between supervised and unsupervised learning.

4. Name the unsupervised tasks.

5. Why are testing and validation important?

6. In one sentence, describe what online learning is.

7. What is the difference between batch and offline learning?

8. Which type of machine learning system should you use to make a robot learn how to walk?

SUMMARY

In this chapter, you've learned many useful concepts, so let's review some concepts that you may feel a bit lost with. Machine learning: ML refers to making machines work better at some task, using given data.

. Machine learning comes in many types, such as supervised, batch, unsupervised, and online learning.

. To perform an ML project, you need to gather data in a training set, and then feed that set to a learning algorithm to get an output, "predictions".

. If you want to get the right output, your system should use clear data, which is not too small and which does not have irrelevant features.

CHAPTER 2

CLASSIFICATION

Installation

You'll need to install Python, Matplotlib and Scikit-learn for this chapter. Just go to the references section and follow the steps indicated.

The MNIST

In this chapter, you'll go deeper into classification systems, and work with the MNIST data set. This is a set of 70,000 images of digits handwritten by students and employees. You'll find that each image has a label and a digit that represents it. This project is like the "Hello, world" example of traditional programming. So every beginner to machine learning should start with this project to learn about the classification algorithm. Scikit-Learn has many functions, including the MNIST. Let's take a look at the code:

```
>>> from sklearn.data sets import fetch_mldata
>>> mn= fetch_mldata('MNIST original')
>>> mn
{'COL_NAMES': ['label', 'data'],
'Description': 'mldata.org data set: mn-original',
'data': array([[0, 0, 0,..., 0, 0, 0],
[0, 0, 0,..., 0, 0, 0],
[0, 0, 0,..., 0, 0, 0],
...,
[0, 0, 0,..., 0, 0, 0],
```

[0, 0, 0,..., 0, 0, 0],
[0, 0, 0,..., 0, 0, 0]], dataType=uint8),
'tar': array([0., 0., 0.,..., 9., 9., 9.])} de

. Description is a key that describes the data set.

. The data key here contains an array with just one row for instance, and a column for every feature.

. This target key contains an array with labels.

Let's work with some of the code:

```
>>> X, y = mn["data"], mn["tar"]
>>> X.shape
(70000, 784)
>>> y.shape
(70000,)
```

. 7000 here means that there are 70,000 images, and every image has more than 700 features: "784". Because, as you can see, every image is 28 x 28 pixels, you can imagine that every pixel is one feature.

Let's take another example from the data set. You'll only need to grab an instance's feature, then make it 26 x 26 arrays, and then display them using the imshow function:

```
%matplotlib inline
import matplotlib
import matplotlib.pyplot as plt
yourDigit = X[36000]
Your_image = your_image.reshape(26, 26)
plt.imshow(Your_image, cmap = matplotlib.cm.binary,
```

interpolation="nearest")
plt.axis("off")
plt.show()

As you can see in the following image, it looks like the number five, and we can give that a label that tells us it's five.

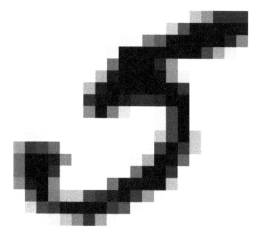

In the following figure, you can see more complex classification tasks from the MNIST data set.

Also, you should create a test set and make it before your data is inspected.

The MNIST data set is divided into two sets, one for training and one for testing.

x_tr, x_tes, y_tr, y_te = x [:60000], x[60000:], y[:60000], y[60000:]

Let's play with your training set as follows to make the cross-validation to be similar (without any missing of any digit)

Import numpy as np

myData = np.radom.permutaion(50000)

x_tr, y_tr = x_tr[myData], y_tr[myData]

Now it's time to make it simple enough, we'll try to just identify one digit, e.g. the number 6. This "6-detector" will be an example of the binary classifier, to distinguish between 6 and not 6, so we'll create the vectors for this task:

Y_tr_6 = (y_tr == 6) // this means it will be true for 6s, and false for any other number

Y_tes_6 = (Y_tes == 6)

After that, we can choose a classifier and train it. Begin with the SGD (Stochastic Gradient Descent) classifier.

The Scikit-Learn class has the advantage of handling very large data sets. In this example, the SGD will deal with instances separately, as follows.

from sklearn.linear_model import SGDClassifier

mycl = SGDClassifier (random_state = 42)

mycl.fit(x_tr, y_tr_6)

to use it to detect the 6

>>>mycl.prdict([any_digit)]

Binary classification:	Multi-class classification:
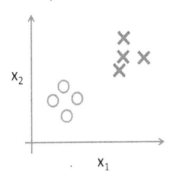	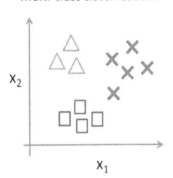

Measures of Performance

If you want to evaluate a classifier, this will be more difficult than a regressor, so let's explain how to evaluate a classifier.

In this example, we'll use across-validation to evaluate our model.

from sklearn.model_selection import StratifiedKFold

form sklearn.base import clone

sf = StratifiedKFold(n=2, ran_state = 40)

for train_index, test_index in sf.split(x_tr, y_tr_6):

cl = clone(sgd_clf)

x_tr_fd = x_tr[train_index]

y_tr_fd = (y_tr_6[train_index])

x_tes_fd = x_tr[test_index]

y_tes_fd = (y_tr_6[test_index])

```
cl.fit(x_tr_fd, y_tr_fd)

y_p = cl.predict(x_tes_fd)

print(n_correct / len(y_p))
```

. We use the **StratifiedFold** class to perform stratified sampling that produces folds that contain a ration for every class. Next, every iteration in the code will create a clone of the classifier to make predictions on the test fold. And finally, it will count the number of correct predictions and their ratio

. Now we'll use the cross_val_score function to evaluate the SGDClassifier by K-fold cross validation. The k fold cross validation will divide the training set into 3 folds, and then it will make prediction and evaluation on each fold.

```
from sklearn.model_selection import cross_val_score

cross_val_score(sgd_clf, x_tr, y_tr_6, cv = 3, scoring = "accuracy")
```

 You'll get the ratio of accuracy of "correct predictions" on all folds.

Let's classify every classifier at every single image in the not-6

```
from sklearn.base import BaseEstimator

class never6Classifier(BaseEstimator):

def fit(self, X, y=None):

  pass
```

```
def predict(self, x):

return np.zeros((len(X), 1), dtype=bool)
```

Let's examine the accuracy of this model with the following code:

```
>>> never_6_cl = Never6Classifier()
>>> cross_val_score(never_6_cl, x_tr, y_tr_6, cv = 3, scoring = "accuracy")
```

Output: array (["num", "num", "num"])

For the output, you'll get no less than 90%: only 10% of the images are 6s, so we can always imagine that an image is not a 6. We'll be right about 90% of the time.

Bear in mind that accuracy is not the best performance measure for classifiers, if you're working with skewed data sets.

Confusion Matrix

There is a better method to evaluate the performance of your classifier: the confusion matrix.

It's easy to measure performance with the confusion matrix, just by counting the number of times instances of class X are classified as class Y, for example. To get the number of times of image classifiers of 6s with 2s, you should look in the 6th row and 2nd column of the confusion matrix.

Let's calculate the confusion matrix using the cross_val_predict () function.

from sklearn.model_selection import cross_Val_predict

y_tr_pre = cross_val_predict (sgd_cl, x_tr, y_tr_6, cv = 3)

This function, like the cross_val_score() function, performs the k fold cross-validation, and it also returns predictions on each fold. It also returns a clean prediction for every instance in your training set.

Now we're ready to get the matrix using the following code.

from sklearn.metrics import confusion_matrix

confusion_matrix (y_tr_6, y_tr_pred)

You'll get an array of 4 values ,"numbers".

Every row represents a class in the matrix, and every column represents a predicted class.

The first row is the negative one: that "contain non-6 images". You can learn a lot from the matrix.

But there is also a good one that's , interesting to work with if you'd like to get the accuracy of the positive predictions, which is the precision of the classifier using this equation.

Precision = (TP)/ (TP+FP)

TP: number of true positives

FP: number of false positives

Recall = (TP) /(TP+FN) "sensitivity": it measure the ratio of positive instances.

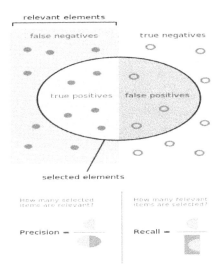

Recall

>>> from sklearn.metrics import precision_score, recall_score

>>> precision_score(y_tr_6, y_pre)

>>>recall_score(y_tr_6, y_tr_pre)

It's very common to combine precision and recall into just one metric, which is the F1 score.

F1 is the mean of both precision and recall. We can calculate the F1 score with the following equation:

F1 = 2 / ((1/precision) + (1)/recall)) = 2 * (precision * recall) / (precision + recall) = (TP) / ((TP) + (FN+FP)/2)

To calculate the F1 score, simply use the following function:

>>> from sklearn.metrics import f1_score

>>>f1_score (y_tr_6, y_pre)

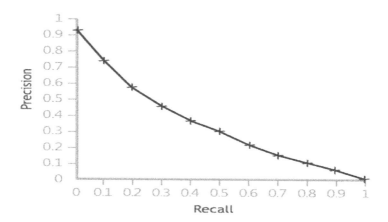

Recall Tradeoff

To get to this point, you should take a look at the SGDClassifier and how it makes decisions regarding classifications. It calculates the score based on the decision function, and then it compares the score with the threshold. If it's greater than this score, it will assign the instance to the "positive or negative". class

For example, if the decision threshold is at the center, you'll find 4 true + on the right side of the threshold, and only one false. So the precision ratio will be only 80%.

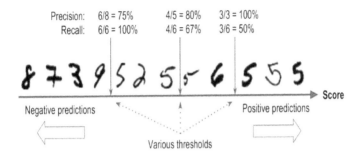

| Precision: | 6/8 = 75% | 4/5 = 80% | 3/3 = 100% |
| Recall: | 6/6 = 100% | 4/6 = 67% | 3/6 = 50% |

Negative predictions · · · · · · · Various thresholds · · · · · · · Positive predictions → Score

In Scikit-Learn, you can't set a threshold directly. You'll need to access the decision scores, which use predictions, and by y calling the decision function, ().

```
>>> y_sco = sgd_clf.decision_funciton([any digit])
```

```
>>> y_sco
```

```
>>> threshold = 0
```

```
>>>y_any_digit_pre = (y_sco > threshold)
```

In this code, the SGDClassifier contains a threshold, = 0, to return the same result as the the predict () function.

```
>>> threshold = 20000
```

```
>>>y_any_digit_pre = (y_sco > threshold)
```

```
>>>y_any_digit_pre
```

This code will confirm that, when the threshold increases, the recall decreases.

y_sco = cross_val_predict (sgd_cl, x_tr, y_tr_6, cv =3, method=”decision function)

It's time to calculate all possible precision and recall for the threshold by calling the precision_recall_curve()function

from sklearn.metrics import precision_recall_curve

precisions, recalls, threshold = precision_recall_curve (y_tr_6, y_sco)

and now let's plot the precision and the recall using Matplotlib

def plot_pre_re(pre, re, thr):

plt.plot(thr, pre[:-1], “b—“, label = “precision”)

plt.plot(thr, re[:1], “g-“, label=”Recall”)

plt.xlabel(“Threshold”)

plt.legend(loc=”left”)

plt.ylim([0,1])

 plot_pre_re(pre, re, thr)

plt.show

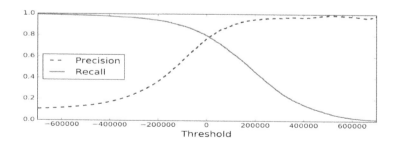

ROC

ROC stands for receiver operating characteristic and it's a tool that used with binary classifiers.

This tool is similar to the recall curve, but it doesn't plot the precision and recall: it plots the positive rate

and false rate. You'll work also with FPR, which is the ratio of negative samples. You can imagine if it's like (1 – negative rate. Another concept is the TNR and it's the specificity. Recall = 1 – specificity.

Let's play with the ROC Curve. First, we'll need to calculate the TPR and the FPR, just by calling the roc-curve () function,

from sklearn.metrics import roc_curve

fp,tp, thers = roc_curve (y_tr_6, y_sco)

After that, you'll plot the FPR and TPR with Matplotlib according to the following instructions.

def_roc_plot (fp, tp, label=none):

plt.plot(fp, tp, linewidth=2, label = label)

plt.plot([0,1)], [0,1], "k--")

plt.axis([0,1,0,1])

plt.xlabel('This is the false rate')

plt.ylabel('This is the true rate')

roc_plot (fp, tp)

plt.show

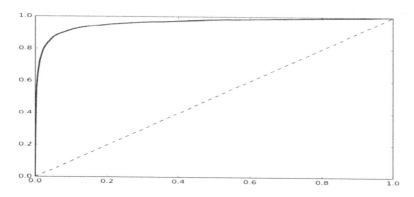

Multi-class Classification

We use binary classifiers to distinguish between any two classes, but what if you'd like to distinguish between more than two?

You can use something like random forest classifiers or Bayes classifiers, which can compare between more than two. But, on the other hand, SVM (the Support Vector Machine) and linear classifiers function like binary classifiers.

If you'd like to develop a system that classifies images of digit into 12 classes (from 0 to 11) you'll need to train 12 binary classifiers, and make one for every classifier (such as 4 – detector, 5-detector, 6-detector and so on), and then you'll need to get the DS, the " decision score," of every classifier for the image. Then, you'll choose the highest score classifier. We call this the OvA strategy: "one-versus-all."

The other method is to train a binary classifier for each pair of digits; for example, one for 5s and 6s and another one for 5s and 7s. — we call this method OvO, "one-versus-one" — to count how many classifiers you'll need, based on the number of classes that use the following equation: "N = number of classes".

N * (N-1)/2. If you'd like to use this technique with the MNIST 10 * (10-1)/2, the output will be 45 classifiers, "binary classifiers".

In Scikit-Learn, you execute OvA automatically when you use a binary classification algorithm.

```
>>> sgd_cl.fit(x_tr, y_tr)
```

```
>>>sgd_cl.Predict([any-digit])
```

Additionally, you can call the decision_function () to return the scores "10 scores for one class"

```
>>>any_digit_scores = sgd_cl.decision_function([any_digit])
```

```
>>> any_digit_scores
```

Array(["num", "num", "num", "num", "num", "num", "num", "num", "num" ,"num"]])

Training a Random Forest Classifier
```
>>> forest.clf.fit(x_tr, y_tr)
```

```
>>> forest.clf.predict([any-digit])
```

```
array([num])
```

As you can see, training a random forest classifierwth only two lines of code is very easy.

The Scikit-Learn didn't execute any OvA or OvO functions because this kind of algorithm — "random forest classifiers" — can automatically work multiple classes. If you'd like to take a look at the list of classifier possibilities, you can call the predict_oroba () function.

>>> forest_cl.predict_proba([any_digit])

array([[0.1, 0, 0, 0.1, 0, 0.8, 0, 0, 0]])

The classifier is very accurate with its prediction, as you can see in the output; there is 0.8 at index number 5.

Let's evaluate the classifier using the cross_val_score() function.

>>> cross_val_score(sgd_cl, x_tr, y_tr, cv=3, scoring = "accuracy")

array([0.84463177, 0.859668, 0.8662669])

You'll get 84% more n the folds. When using a random classifier, you'll get, in this case, 10% for the accuracy score. Keep in mind that the higher this value is, the better.

Error Analysis
First of all, when developing a machine learning project:

1. Determine the problem;
2. Collect your data;
3. Work on your data and explore it;
4. Clean the data
5. Work with several models and choose the best one;
6. Combine your models into the solution;
7. Show your solution;
8. Execute and test your system.

First, you should work with the confusion matrix and make predictions
by the cross-val function. Next, you'll call the confusion matrix
function:

>>> y_tr_pre = cross_val_prediciton(sgd_cl, x_tr_scaled, y_tr, cv=3)
>>> cn_mx = confusion_matrix(y_tr, y_tr_pre)
>>> cn_mx

array([[5625, 2, 25, 8, 11, 44, 52, 12, 34, 6],

[2, 2415, 41, 22, 8, 45, 10, 10, 9],

[52, 43, 7443, 104, 89, 26, 87, 60, 166, 13],

[47, 46, 141, 5342, 1, 231, 40, 50, 141, 92],

[19, 29, 41, 10, 5366, 9, 56, 37, 86, 189],

[73, 45, 36, 193, 64, 4582, 111, 30, 193, 94],

[29, 34, 44, 2, 42, 85, 5627, 10, 45, 0],

[25, 24, 74, 32, 54, 12, 6, 5787, 15, 236],

[52, 161, 73, 156, 10, 163, 61, 25, 5027, 123],

[50, 24, 32, 81, 170, 38, 5, 433, 80, 4250]])

Plt.matshow(cn_mx, cmap=plt.cm.gray)

Plt.show()

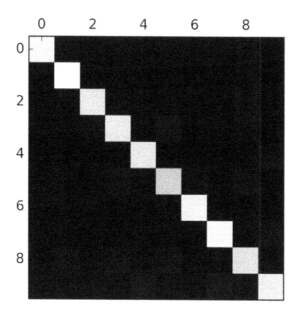

First, you should divide every value in the matrix by the number of images in the class, and then you'll compare the error rates.

rw_sm = cn_mx.sum(axis=1, keepdims=True)

nm_cn_mx = cn_mx / rw_sum

The next step is to **make all the zeros on the diagonal,** and that will keep the errors from occurring.

np.fill_diagonal (nm_cn_mx, 0)

plt.matshow(nm_cn_mx, cmap=plt.cm.gray)

plt.show()

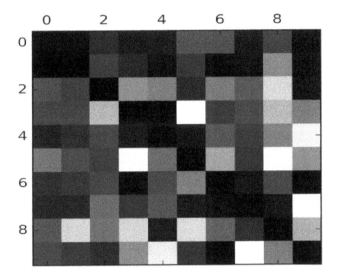

The errors are easy to spot in the above schema. One thing to keep in mind is that the rows represent classes and the columns represent the predicted values.

Multi-label Classifications

In the above examples, every class has just one instance. But what if we want to assign the instances to multiple classes — face recognition, for example. Suppose that you'd like to find more than one face in the same photo. There will be one label for each face. Let's practice with a simple example.

y_tr_big = (y_tr >= 7)

y_tr_odd = (y_tr %2 ==1)

y_multi = np.c [y_tr_big, y_tr_odd]

kng_cl = KNeighborsClassifier()

kng_cl.fit (x_tr, y_m,ulti)

In these instructions, we have created a y_mullti array that contains two labels for every image.

And the first one contains information on whether the digit is "big" (8,9,.), and the second one checks if it's odd or not.

Next, we'll make a prediction using the following set of instructions.

>>>kng_cl.predict([any-digit])

Array([false, true], dataType=bool)

True here means that it's odd and **false,** that it's not big.

Multi-output Classification

At this point, we can cover the final type of classification task, which is the multi-output classification.

It's just a general case of multi-label classification, but every label will have a multiclass. In other words, it will have more than one value.

Let's make it clear with this example, using the MNIST images, and adding some noise to the image with the NumPy functions.

No = rnd.randint (0, 101, (len(x_tr), 785)))

No = rnd.randint(0, 101, (len(x_tes), 785))

x_tr_mo = x_tr + no

x_tes_mo = x_tes + no

y_tr_mo = x_tr

y_tes_mo = x_tes

kng_cl.fit(x_tr_mo, y_tr_mo)

cl_digit = kng_cl.predict(x_tes_mo[any-index]])

plot_digit(cl_digit)

1. Construct a classifier for the MNIST data set . Try to get more than 96% accuracy on your test set.

2. Write a method to shift an image from the MNIST (right or left) by 2 pixels.

3. Develop your own anti-spam program or classifier.

-   Download examples of spam from Google.

-   Extract the data set.

-   Divide the data set into training for a test set.

-   Write a program to convert every email to a feature vector.

- Play with the classifiers, and try to construct the best one possible, with high values for recall and precision.

SUMMARY

In this chapter, you've learned useful new concepts and implemented many types of classification algorithms. You've also worked with new concepts, like :

- ROC: the receiver operating characteristic, the tool used with binary classifiers.

- Error Analysis: optimizing your algorithms.

- How to train a random forest classifier using the forest function in Scikit-Learn.

- Understanding Multi-Output Classification.

- Understanding multi-Label classifications.

REFERENCES

http://scikit-learn.org/stable/install.html

https://www.python.org

https://matplotlib.org/2.1.0/users/installing.html

http://yann.lecun.com/exdb/mnist/

CHAPTER 3

HOW TO TRAIN A MODEL

After working with many machine learning models and training algorithms, which seem like unfathomable black boxes. we were able to optimize a regression system, have also worked with image classifiers. But we developed these systems without understanding what's s inside and how they work, so now we need to go deeper so that we can grasp how they work and understand the details of implementation.

Gaining a deep understanding of these details will help you with the right model and with choosing the best training algorithm. Also, it will help you with debugging and error analysis.

In this chapter, we'll work with polynomial regression, which is a complex model that works for nonlinear data sets. In addition, we'll working with several regularization techniques that reduce training that encourages overfitting.

Linear Regression

As an example, we'll take l_S = $\theta 0$ + $\theta 1$ × GDP_per_cap. This is a simple model for a linear function of the input feature ,"GPD_per_cap". ($\theta 0$ and $\theta 1$) are the parameters of the model,

In general, you'll use a linear model to make a prediction by calculating a weighted sum of the input features, and also a constant "bias," as you can see in the following equation.

$$\hat{y} = \theta_0 + \theta_1 x_1 + \theta_2 x_2 + \cdots + \theta_n x_n$$

. Y is the value of the predictor.

. N represents the features

. X1 is the value of the feature.

. Θj is the model parameter of j theta.

Also, we can write the equation in vectorized form, as in the following example:

$$\hat{y} = h_\theta(x) = \theta^T \cdot x$$

. Θ is the value that minimizes the cost.

. Y contains the values y (1) to y (m).

Let's write some code to practice.

Import numpy as np

V1_x = 2 * np.random.rand (100, 1)

V2_y = 4 + 3 * V1_x + np.random.randn (100, 1)

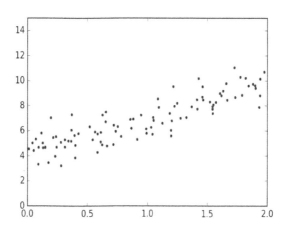

After that, we'll calculate Θ value using our equation. It's time to use the inv() function from our linear algebra module of numpy (np.linalg)to calculate the inverse of any matrix, and also, the dot() function for multiply our matrix

Value1 = np.c_[np.ones((100, 1)), V1_x]

myTheta =
np.linalg.inv(Value1.T.dot(Value1)).dot(Value1.T).dot(V2_y)

>>>myTheta

Array([[num], [num]])

This function uses the following equation — y = 4 + 3x + noise "Gaussian" — to generate our data.

Now let's make our predictions.

>>>V1_new = np.array([[0],[2]])

>>>V1_new_2 = np.c_[np.ones((2,1)), V1_new]

>>>V2_predicit = V1_new_2.dot(myTheta)

>>>V2_predict

Array([[4.219424], [9.74422282]])

Now, it's time to plot the model.

Plt.plot(V1_new, V2_predict, "r-")

Plt.plot(V1_x, V2_y, "b.")

Plt.axis([0,2,0,15])

Plt.show()

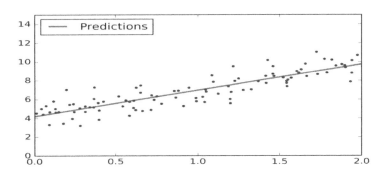

Computational Complexity

With the normal formula, we can compute the inverse of $M^T . M$ — that is, a $n*n$ matrix (n = the number of features). The complexity of this inversion is something like $O(n^{2.5})$ to $O(n^{3.2})$, which is based on the implementation. Actually, **if you make the number of features**

like twice, you'll make the time of the computation attain between 2^2.5 and 2^3.2.

The great news here is that the equation is a linear equation. This means It can easily handle huge training sets and fit the memory in.

After training your model, the predictions will be not slow, and the complexity will be simple, thanks to the linear model. It's time to go deeper into the methods of training a linear regression model, which is always used when there is a large number of features and instances in the memory.

Gradient Descent

This algorithm is a general algorithm that is used for optimization and for providing the optimal solution for various problems. The idea of this algorithm is to work with the parameters in an iterative way, to make the cost function as simple as possible.

The gradient descent algorithm calculates the gradient of the error using the parameter theta, and it works with the method of descending gradient. If the gradient is equal to zero, you'll reach the minimum.

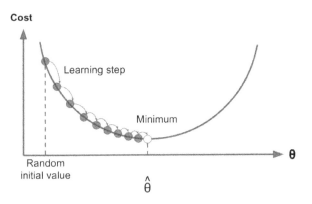

Also, you should keep in the mind that the size of the steps is very important for this algorithm, because if it's very small – "meaning the rate of learning" is slow – it will take a long time to cover everything that it needs to.

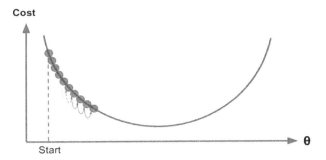

But when the rate of learning is high, It will take short time to cover what's needed, and it will provide an optimal solution.

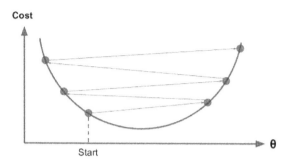

At the end, you won't always find that all cost functions are easy, as you can see, but you'll also find irregular functions that make getting an optimal solution very difficult. This problem occurs when the local minimum and global minimum looks like they do in the following figure.

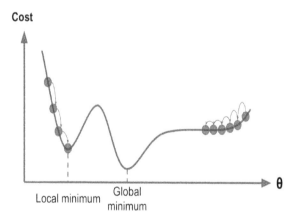

If you assign any to any two points on your curve, you'll find that the segment of the line won't join them on the same curve. This cost function will look like a bowl, which will occur if the features have many scales, as n the following image

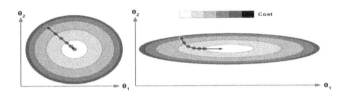

Batch Gradient Descent

If you'd like to implement this algorithm, you should first calculate the gradient of your cost function using the theta parameter. If the value of the parameter theta has changed, you'll need to know the changing rate of your cost function. We can call this change by a partial derivative

We can calculate the partial derivative using the following equation:

$$\frac{\partial}{\partial \theta_j} \text{MSE}(\theta) = \frac{2}{m} \sum_{i=1}^{m} (\theta^T \cdot x^{(i)} - y^{(i)}) x_j^{(i)}$$

But we`ll also use the following equation to calculate the partial derivatives and the gradient vector together.

$$\nabla_\theta \, \text{MSE}\, (\theta) = \begin{pmatrix} \frac{\partial}{\partial \theta_0} \, \text{MSE}\, (\theta) \\ \frac{\partial}{\partial \theta_1} \, \text{MSE}\, (\theta) \\ \vdots \\ \frac{\partial}{\partial \theta_n} \, \text{MSE}\, (\theta) \end{pmatrix} = \frac{2}{m} X^T \cdot (X \cdot \theta - y)$$

Let's implement the algorithm.

Lr = 1 # Lr for learning rate

Num_it = 1000 # number of iterations

L = 100

myTheta = np.random.randn (2,1)

for it in range(Num_it):

gr = 2/L * Value1.T.dot(Value1.dot(myTheta) – V2_y)

myTheta = myTheta – Lr * gr

>>> myTheta

Array([[num],[num]])

If you try to change the learning rate value, you'll get different shapes, as in the following figure.

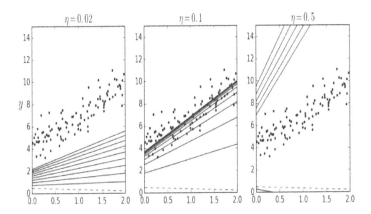

Stochastic Gradient Descent

You'll find a problem when you're using the batch gradient descent: it needs to use the whole training set in order to calculate the value at each step, and that will affect performance "speed".

But when using the stochastic gradient descent, the algorithm will randomly choose an instance from your training set at each step, and then it will calculate the value. In this way, the algorithm will be faster than the batch gradient descent, since it doesn't need to use the whole set to calculate the value. On the other hand, because of the randomness of this method, it will be irregular when compared to the batch algorithm.

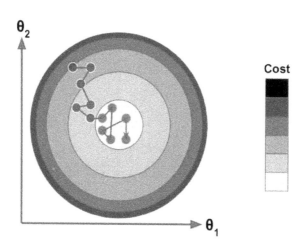

Let's implement the algorithm.

Nums = 50

L1, L2 = 5, 50

Def lr_sc(s):

   return L1 / (s + L2)

myTheta = np.random.randn(2,1)

for Num in range (Nums):

for l in range (f)

myIndex = np.random.randint(f)

V1_Xi = Value1[myIndex:myIndex+1]

V2_yi = V2_y[myIndex:myIndex+1]

gr = 2 * V1_xi.T.dot(V1_xi.dot(myTheta) – V2_yi)

Lr = lr_sc(Num * f + i)

myTheta = myTheta – Lr * gr

>>> myTheta

Array ([[num], [num]])

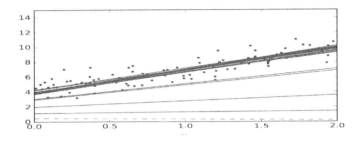

Mini-Batch Gradient Descent

Because you already know the batch and the stochastic algorithms, this kind of algorithms is very easy to understand and work with . As you know, both algorithms calculate the value of the gradients, based on the whole training set or just one instance. However, the mini-batch calculates its algorithms based on small and random sets, and performs better than the other two algorithms.

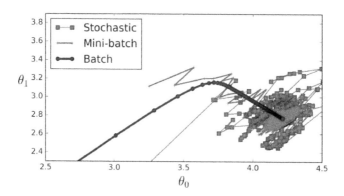

Polynomial Regression

We'll use this technique when working with more complex data, especially, in the case of linear and nonlinear data. After we've added the powers of every feature, we can train the model with new features. This is known as polynomial regression.

Now, let's write some code.

L = 100

V1 = 6*np.random.rand(L, 1) – 3

V2 = 0.5 * V1**2 + V1 + 2 + np.random.randn(L, 1)

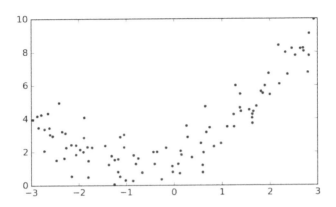

As you can see. the straight will never represent the data in the most efficient way. So we'll use the polynomial method to work on this problem.

>>>from sklearn.preprocession import PolynomialFeatures

>>>P_F = PolynomialFeatures(degree = 2, include_bias=False)

>>>V1_P = P_F.fit_transform(V1)

>>>V1[0]

Array([num])

>>>V1_P[0]

Now, let's make this function properly with our data, and change the straight line.

>>> ln_r = LinearRegression()

```
>>>ln_r.fit(V1_P, V2)

>>>ln_r.intercept_, ln_r.coef
```

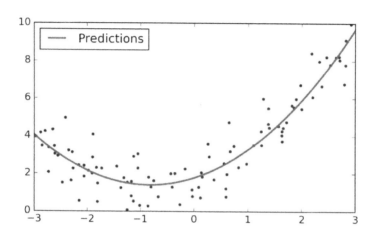

Learning Curves

Assume that you're work with polynomial regression, and you want it to fit the data better than with the linear one . In the following image, you'll find a 300-degree model . We can also compare the final result with the other kind of the regression: "normal linear".

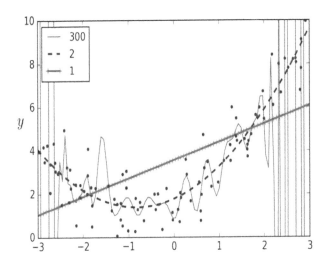

In the above figure, you can see the overfitting of data when you're using the polynomial. On the other hand, with linear one, you can see that the data is obviously being underfitted.

Regularized Linear Models

We have worked, in the first and second chapters, on how to reduce overfitting by regularizing the model a little, as an example, if you'd like to regularize a polynomial model. In this case, to fix the problem, you should decrease the number of degrees.

Ridge Regression

The ridge regression is another version of the linear regression, but, after regularizing it and adding weight to the cost function, this makes it fit the data, and even makes the weight of the model as simple as possible. Here is the cost function of the ridge regression:

$$J(\theta) = \text{MSE}(\theta) + \alpha\frac{1}{2}\sum_{i=1}^{n}\theta_i^2$$

As an example of ridge regression, just take a look at the following figures.

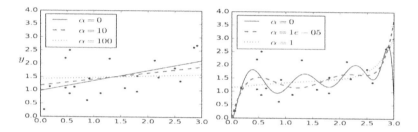

Lasso Regression

"Lasso" regression stands for "Least Absolute Shrinkage and Selection Operator" regression. This is another type of the regularized version of linear regression.

It looks like ridge regression, but with a small difference in the equation, as in the following figures

The cost function of the lasso regression:

$$J(\theta) = \text{MSE}(\theta) + \alpha \sum_{i=1}^{n} |\theta_i|$$

As you can see in the following figure, the lasso regression uses smaller values than the ridge.

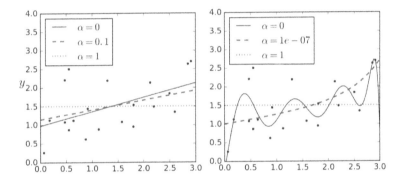

1. If you have a set that contains a huge number of features (millions of them), which regression algorithm should you use, and why?

2. If you use batch gradient descent to plot the error at each period, and suddenly the rate of errors increases, how would you fix this problem?

3. What should you do if you notice that errors become larger when you're using the mini-batch method? Why?

4. From these pairs, which method is better? Why? :

. Ridge regression and linear regression?

. Lasso regression and ridge regression?

5. Write the batch Gradient descent algorithm.

SUMMARY

In this chapter, you've learned new concepts, and have learned how to train a model using different types of algorithms. You've also learned when to use each algorithm, including the following:

- Batch gradient descent

- Mini-batch gradient descent

- Polynomial regression

- Regularized linear models
  . Ridge regression

    . Lasso regression

In addition, you now know the meaning of certain terms: linear regression, computational complexity, and gradient descent.

Chapter 4

Different models combinations

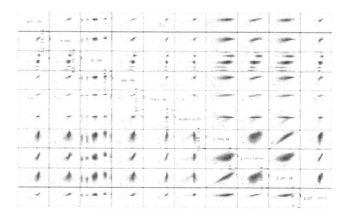

Tree classifers.

The next image will illustrate the definition of a general target of collecting functions that is just to merge different classifers into a One-classifer that has a better generalization performance than each individual classifer alone.

As an example, assume that you collected predictions from many experts. Ensemble methods would allow us to merge these predictions by the lots of experts to get a prediction that is more proper and robust than the predictions of each individual expert. As you can see later in this part, there are many different methods to create an ensemble of classifers. In this part, we will introduce a basic perception about how ensembles work and why they are typically recognized for yielding a good generalization performance.

In this part, we will work with the most popular ensemble method that uses the majority voting principle. Many voting simply means that we choose the label that has been predicted by the majority of classifers; that is, received more than 50 percent of the votes. As an example, the term here is like vote refers to just binary class settings only. However, it is not hard to generate the majority voting principle to multi-class settings, which is called plurality voting. After that, we will choose the class label that received the most votes. The following diagram illustrates the concept of majority and plurality voting for an ensemble of 10 classifers where each unique symbol (triangle, square, and circle) represents a unique class label:

Using the training set, we start by training m different classifers (C C 1, , ... m). Based on the method, the ensemble can be built from many classification algorithms; for example, decision trees, support vector machines, logistic regression classifers, and so on. In fact, you can use the same base classification algorithm fitting different subsets of the training set. An example of this method would be the random forest algorithm, which merges many decision ensemble ways using majority voting.

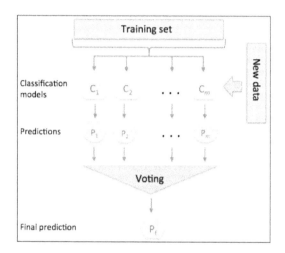

To predict a class label via a simple majority or plurality voting, we combine the predicted class labels of each individual classifer C j and select the class label y^ that received the most votes:

$$y\ m\ \hat{} = ode\{C\ C\ 1\ 2\ ()\ \mathbf{x}\ \mathbf{x}\ ,\ ,\ ()\ ...,Cm\ ()\ \mathbf{x}\}$$

For example, in a binary classification task where class1 $1 = -$ and class2 $1 = +$, we can write the majority vote prediction.

To illustrate why ensemble methods can work better than individual classifiers alone, let's apply the simple concepts of combinatory. For the following example, we make the assumption that all n base classifiers for a binary classification task have an equal error rate, ε. Additionally, we assume that the classifiers are independent and the error rates are not correlated. As you can see, we can simply explain the error statistics of an ensemble of base classifiers as a probability.

Mass function of a binomial distribution:

Here, n. k is the binomial coefficient n choose k. As you can see, you can calculate the probability that the prediction of the ensemble is wrong. Now, let's take a look at a more concrete example of 11 base classifiers (n =11) with an error rate of 0.25 (ε = 0.25):

You can notice that the error rate of the ensemble (0.034) is smaller than the error rate of each individual classifer (0.25) if all the assumptions are met. Note that in this simplified image, a 50-50 split by an even number of classifiers n is treated as an error, whereas this is only true half of the time. To compare such an idealistic ensemble classifer to a base classifer over a range of different base error rates, let's implement the probability mass function in Python:

```
>>> import math

>>> def ensemble_error(n_classifier, error):

... q_start = math.ceil(n_classifier / 2.0)

... Probability = [comb(n_class, q) *

... error**q *

... (1-error)**(n_classifier - q)
```

```
...          for q in range(q_start, l_classifier + 2)]

...     return sum(Probability)

>>> ensemble_error(n_classifier=11, error=0.25)

0.034327507019042969
```

Let's write some code to compute the rates for the different errors visualize the relationship between ensemble and base errors in a line graph:

```
>>> import numpy as np

>>> error_range = np.arange(0.0, 1.01, 0.01)

>>> en_error = [en_er(n_classifier=11, er=er)

...     for er in er_range]

>>> import matplotlib.pyplot as plt

>>> plt.plot(er_range, en_error,

...     label='Ensemble error',

...     linewidth=2)

>>> plt.plot(er_range, er_range,

...     ls='--', label='B_ er',
```

```
... linewidth=2)

>>> plt.xlabel('B_ er')

>>> plt.label('B/En_er')

>>> plt.legend(loc='upper left')

>>> plt.grid()

>>> plt.show()
```

As we can see in the resulting plot, the error probability of an ensemble is always better than the error of an individual base classifer as long as the base classifiers perform better than random guessing ($\varepsilon < 0.5$). You should notice that the y-axis depicts the base error as well as the ensemble error (continuous line):

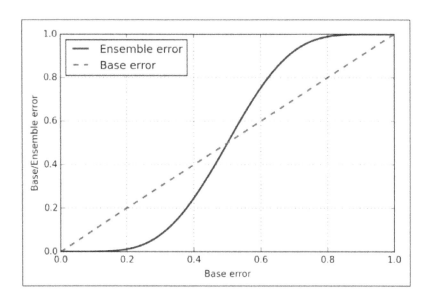

Implementing a simple majority classifer

As we saw in the introduction to merge learning in the last section, we will work with a warm-up training and then develop a simple classifer for majority voting in Python programming. As you can see, the next algorithm will work on multi-class settings via plurality voting; you will use the term majority voting for simplicity as is also often done in literature.

In the following program, we will develop and also combine different classification programs associated with individual weights for confidence. Our goal is to build a stronger meta-classifer that balances out the individual classifiers' weaknesses on a particular dataset. In more precise mathematical terms, we can write the weighted majority vote.

To translate the concept of the weighted majority vote into Python code, we can use NumPy's convenient argmax and bincount functions:

```
>>> import numpy as np

>>> np.argmax(np.bincount([0, 0, 1],

... weights=[0.2, 0.2, 0.6]))

1
```

Here, p_{ij} is the predicted probability of the jth classifer for class label i. To continue with our previous example, let's assume that we have a binary classification problem with class labels $i \in \{\} 0,1$ and an ensemble of three classifiers C_j ($j \in \{\} 1,2,3$). Let's assume that the classifer C_j returns the following class membership probabilities for a particular sample x:

C_1 () x $\rightarrow$ [] 0.9,0.1 , C_2 () x $\rightarrow$ [] 0.8,0.2 , C_3 () x $\rightarrow$ [] 0.4,0.6

To implement the weighted majority vote based on class probabilities, we can again make use of NumPy using numpy.average and np.argmax:

```
>>> ex = np.array([[0.9, 0.1],

... [0.8, 0.2],

... [0.4, 0.6]])
```

```
>>> p = np.average(ex, axis=0, weights=[0.2, 0.2, 0.6])

>>> p

array([ 0.58, 0.42])

>>> np.argmax(p)

0
```

Putting everything together, let's now implement a MajorityVoteClassifier in Python:

```
from sklearn.base import ClassifierMixin

from sklearn.pre_processing import Label_En

from sklearn.ext import six

from sklearn.ba import clone

from sklearn.pipeline import _name_estimators

import numpy as np

import operator

class MVClassifier(BaseEstimator,

ClassifierMixin):

""" A majority vote ensemble classifier
```

Parameters

----

cl : array-like, shape = [n_classifiers]

Different classifiers for the ensemble vote: str, {'cl_label', 'prob'}

Default: 'cl_label'

If 'cl_label' the prediction is based on the argmax of class labels. Elif 'prob', the arg of the total of probs is used to predict the class label (recommended for calibrated classifiers).

w : arr-like, s = [n_cl]

Optional, default: None

If a list of `int` or `float` values are provided, the classifiers are weighted by """

def __init__(s, cl,

v='cl_label', w=None):

s.cl = cl

s.named_cl = {key: value for

key, value in

_name_estimators(cl)}

```python
s.v = v

s.w= w

def fit_cl(s, X, y):

    """ Fit_cl.

    Parameters

    ----------

    X : {array-like, sparse matrix},

    s = [n_samples, n_features]

    Matrix of training samples.

    y : arr_like, sh = [n_samples]

    Vector of target class labels.

    Returns

    -------

    s : object

    """

    # Use LabelEncoder to ensure class labels start

    # with 0, which is important for np.argmax
```

```
# call in s.predict

s.l_ = LabelEncoder()

s.l_.fit(y)

s.cl_ = self.lablenc_.classes_

s.cl_ = []

for cl in s.cl:

fit_cl = clone(cl).fit(X,

s.la_.transform(y))

s.cl_.append(fit_cl)

return s
```

I added a lot of comments to the code to better understand the individual parts. However, before we implement the remaining methods, let's take a quick break and discuss some of the code that may look confusing at first. We used the parent classes BaseEstimator and ClassifierMixin to get some base functionality for free, including the methods get_params and set_params to set and return the classifer's parameters as well as the score method to calculate the prediction accuracy, respectively. Also, note that we imported six to make the MajorityVoteClassifier compatible with Python 2.7.

Next, we will add the predict method to predict the class label via majority vote based on the class labels if we initialize a new MajorityVoteClassifier object with vote='classlabel'. Alternatively, we will be able to initialize the ensemble classifer with vote='probability' to predict the class label based on the class membership probabilities. Furthermore, we will also add a predict_proba method to return the average probabilities, which is useful to compute the Receiver Operator Characteristic area under the curve (ROC AUC).

def pre(s, X):

""" Pre class labels for X.

Parameters

X : {arr-like, spar mat},

Sh = [n_samples, n_features]

Matrix of training samples.

Returns

----

ma_v : arr-like, sh = [n_samples]

Predicted class labels.

```python
"""

if se.v == 'probability':

ma_v = np.argmax(spredict_prob(X),

axis=1)

else: # 'cl_label' v

predictions = np.asarr([cl.predict(X)

for cl in

s.cl_]).T

ma_v = np.ap_al_ax(

lambda x:

np.argmax(np.bincount(x, weights=s.w)),

axis=1,

arr=predictions)

ma_v = s.l_.inverse_transform(ma_v)

return ma_v

def predict_proba(self, X):

""" Prediction for X.
```

Parameters

X : {arr-like, sp mat},

sh = [n_samples, n_features]

Training vectors, where n_samples is the number of samples and n_features is the number of features.

Returns

----

av_prob : array-like,

sh = [n_samples, n_classes]

Weighted average probability for each class per sample.

"""

probs = np.asarr([cl.predict_prob(X)

for cl in s.cl_])

av_prob = np.av(probs,

axis=0, weights=s.w)

return av_prob

```python
def get_ps(self, deep=True):

    """ Get classifier parameter names for GridSearch"""

    if not deep:

        return super(MVC,

        self).get_ps(deep=False)

    else:

        ou = s.n_cl.copy()

        for n, step in\

        six.iteritems(s.n_cl):

            for k, value in six.iteritems(

            step.get_ps(deep=True)):

                ou['%s__%s' % (n, k)] = value

        return ou
```

Combining different algorithms for classification with majority vote

Now, it is about time to put the MVC that we implemented in the previous section into action. You should first prepare a dataset that you can test it on. Since we are already familiar with techniques to load datasets from CSV files, we will take a shortcut and load the Iris dataset from scikit-learn's dataset module.

Furthermore, we will only select two features, sepal width and petal length, to make the classification task more challenging. Although our MajorityVoteClassifier, or MVC, generalizes to multiclass problems, we will only classify flower samples from the two classes, Ir-Versicolor and Ir-Virginica, to compute the ROC AUC. The code is as follows:

```
>>> import sklearn as sk

>>> import sklearn.cross_validation as cv

>>> ir = datasets.load_ir()

>>> X, y = ir.data[50:, [1, 2]], ir.target[50:]

>>> le = LabelEncoder()

>>> y = le.fit_transform(y)
```

Next we split the Iris samples into 50 percent training and 50 percent test data:

```
>>> X_train, X_test, y_train, y_test =\

... train_test_split(X, y,

... test_size=0.5,

... random_state=1)
```

Using the training dataset, we now will train three different classifiers — a logistic regression classifier, a decision tree classifer, and a k-nearest neighbors classifier — and look at their individual performances via a 10 cross-validation on the training dataset before we merge them into an ensemble one:

import the following

sklearn.cross_validation

sklearn.linear_model

sklearn.tree

sklearn.pipeline

Pipeline

numpy as np

```
>>> clf1 = LogisticRegression(penalty='l2',

... C=0.001,
```

```
... random_state=0)

>>> clf2 = DTCl(max_depth=1,

... criterion='entropy',

... random_state=0)


>>> cl = KNC(n_nb=1,

... p=2,

... met='minsk')

>>> pipe1 = Pipeline([['sc', StandardScaler()],

... ['clf', clf1]])

>>> pipe3 = Pipeline([['sc', StandardScaler()],

... ['clf', clf3]])

>>> clf_labels = ['Logistic Regression', 'Decision Tree', 'KNN']

>>> print('10-fold cross validation:\n')

>>> for clf, label in zip([pipe1, clf2, pipe3], clf_labels):

... sc = crossVSc(estimator=clf,

>>> X=X_train,
```

```
>>> y=y_train,

>>> cv=10,

>>> scoring='roc_auc')

>>> print("ROC AUC: %0.2f (+/- %0.2f) [%s]"

... % (scores.mean(), scores.std(), label))
```

The output that we receive, as shown in the following snippet, shows that the

predictive performances of the individual classifiers are almost equal:

10-fold cross validation:

ROC AUC: 0.92 (+/- 0.20) [Logistic Regression]

ROC AUC: 0.92 (+/- 0.15) [Decision Tree]

ROC AUC: 0.93 (+/- 0.10) [KNN]

You may be wondering why we trained the logistic regression and k-nearest neighbors classifier as part of a pipeline. The cause here is that, as we said, logistic regression and k-nearest neighbors algorithms (using the Euclidean distance metric) are not scale-invariant in contrast with decision trees. However, the Ir advantages are all measured on the same scale; it is a good habit to work with standardized features.

Now, let's move on to the more exciting part and combine the individual classifiers for majority rule voting in our M_V_C:

```
>>> mv_cl = M_V_C(

... cl=[pipe1, clf2, pipe3])

>>> cl_labels += ['Majority Voting']

>>> all_cl = [pipe1, clf2, pipe3, mv_clf]

>>> for cl, label in zip(all_clf, clf_labels):

... sc = cross_val_score(est=cl,

... X=X_train,

... y=y_train,

... cv=10,

... scoring='roc_auc')

... % (scores.mean(), scores.std(), label))

R_AUC: 0.92 (+/- 0.20) [Logistic Regression]

R_AUC: 0.92 (+/- 0.15) [D_T]

R_AUC: 0.93 (+/- 0.10) [KNN]

R_AUC: 0.97 (+/- 0.10) [Majority Voting]
```

Additionally, the output of the MajorityVotingClassifier has substantially improved over the individual classifiers in the 10-fold cross-validation evaluation.

Classifier

In this part, you are going to compute the R_C curves from the test set to check if the MV_Classifier generalizes well to unseen data. We should remember that the test set will not be used for model selection; the only goal is to report an estimate of the accuracy of a classifer system. Let's take a look at Import metrics.

import roc_curve from sklearn.metrics import auc

cls = ['black', 'orange', 'blue', 'green']

ls = [':', '--', '-.', '-']

 for cl, label, cl, l \

... in zip(all_cl, cl_labels, cls, ls):

... y_pred = clf.fit(X_train,

... y_train).predict_proba(X_test)[:, 1]

... fpr, tpr, thresholds = rc_curve(y_t=y_tes,

... y_sc=y_pr)

... rc_auc = ac(x=fpr, y=tpr)

```
... plt.plot(fpr, tpr,
... color=clr,
... linestyle=ls,
... la='%s (ac = %0.2f)' % (la, rc_ac))
>>> plt.lg(lc='lower right')
>>> plt.plot([0, 1], [0, 1],
... linestyle='--',
... color='gray',
... linewidth=2)
>>> plt.xlim([-0.1, 1.1])
>>> plt.ylim([-0.1, 1.1])
>>> plt.grid()
>>> plt.xlb('False Positive Rate')
>>> plt.ylb('True Positive Rate')
>>> plt.show()
```

As we can see in the resulting ROC, the ensemble classifer also performs well on the test set (ROC AUC = 0.95), whereas the k-nearest neighbors classifer seems to be over-fitting the training data (training ROC AUC = 0.93, test ROC AUC = 0.86):

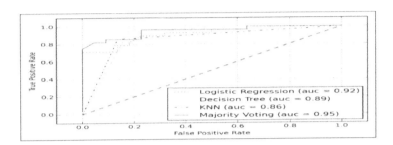

You only choose two features for the classification tasks. It will be interesting to show what the decision region of the ensemble classifer actually looks like. Although it is not necessary to standardize the training features prior to model to fit because our logistic regression and k-nearest neighbors pipelines will automatically take care of this, you will make the training set so that the decision regions of the decision tree will be on the same scale for visual purposes.

Let's take a look:

>>> sc = SS()

X_tra_std = sc.fit_transform(X_train)

From itertools import product

x_mi= X_tra_std[:, 0].mi() - 1

x_ma = X_tra_std[:, 0].ma() + 1

97

```python
y_mi = X_tra_std[:, 1].mi() - 1

y_ma = X_tra_std[:, 1].ma() + 1

xx, yy = np.meshgrid(np.arange(x_min, x_max, 0.1),

... np.arange(y_mi, y_ma, 0.1))

f, axarr = plt.subplots(nrows=2, ncols=2,

sharex='col',

sharey='row',

figze=(7, 5))

for ix, cl, tt in zip(product([0, 1], [0, 1]),

all_cl, cl_lb):

... cl.fit(X_tra_std, y_tra)

... Z = clf.predict(np.c_[xx.ravel(), yy.ravel()])

... Z = Z.resh(xx.shape)

... axarr[idx[0], idx[1]].contou(_xx, _yy, Z, alph=0.3)

... axarr[idx[0], idx[1]].scatter(X_tra_std[y_tra==0, 0],

... X_tra_std[y_tra==0, 1],

... c='blue',
```

```
... mark='^',

... s=50)

... axarr[idx[0], idx[1]].scatt(X_tra_std[y_tra==1, 0],

... X_tra_std[y_tra==1, 1],

... c='red',

... marker='o',

... s=50)

... axarr[idx[0], idx[1]].set_title(tt)

>>> plt.text(-3.5, -4.5,

... z='Sl wid [standardized]',

... ha='center', va='center', ftsize=12)

>>> plt.text(-10.5, 4.5,

... z='P_length [standardized]',

... ha='center', va='center',

... f_size=13, rotation=90)

>>> plt.show()
```

Interestingly, but also as expected, the decision regions of the ensemble classifier seem to be a hybrid of the decision regions from the individual classifiers. At first glance, the majority vote decision boundary looks a lot like the decision boundary of the k-nearest neighbor classifier. However, we can see that it is orthogonal to the y axis for sepal width ≥1, just like the decision tree stump:

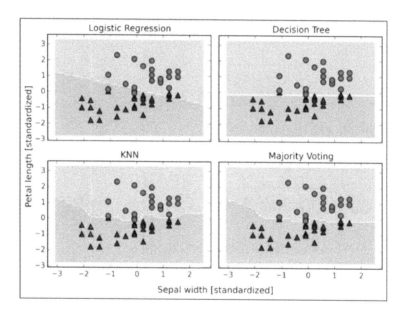

Before you learn how to tune the individual classifer parameters for ensemble classification, let's call the get_ps method to find an essential idea of how we can access the individual parameters inside a GridSearch object:

>>> mv_clf.get_params()

```
{'decisiontreeclassifier': DecisionTreeClassifier(class_weight=None,

criterion='entropy', max_depth=1,

max_features=None, max_leaf_nodes=None, min_samples_

leaf=1,

min_samples_split=2, min_weight_fraction_leaf=0.0,

random_state=0, splitter='best'),

'decisiontreeclassifier__class_weight': None,

'decisiontreeclassifier__criterion': 'entropy',

[...]

'decisiontreeclassifier__random_state': 0,

'decisiontreeclassifier__splitter': 'best',

'pipeline-1': Pipeline(steps=[('sc', StandardScaler(copy=True, with_

mean=True, with_std=True)), ('clf', LogisticRegression(C=0.001,
class_

weight=None, dual=False, fit_intercept=True,

intercept_scaling=1, max_iter=100, multi_class='ovr',

penalty='l2', random_state=0, solver='liblinear',
```

tol=0.0001,

verbose=0))]),

'pipeline-1__clf': LogisticRegression(C=0.001, class_weight=None,

dual=False, fit_intercept=True,

intercept_scaling=1, max_iter=100, multi_class='ovr',

penalty='l2', random_state=0, solver='liblinear',

tol=0.0001,

verbose=0),

'pipeline-1__clf__C': 0.001,

'pipeline-1__clf__class_weight': None,

'pipeline-1__clf__dual': False,

[...]

'pipeline-1__sc__with_std': True,

'pipeline-2': Pipeline(steps=[('sc', StandardScaler(copy=True, with_

mean=True, with_std=True)), ('clf',
KNeighborsClassifier(algorithm='au

to', leaf_size=30, metric='minkowski',

metric_params=None, n_neighbors=1, p=2,

w='uniform'))]),

'p-2__cl": KNC(algorithm='auto', leaf_

size=30, met='miski',

met_ps=None, n_neighbors=1, p=2,

w='uniform'),

'p-2__cl__algorithm': 'auto',

[...]

'p-2__sc__with_std': T}

Depending on the values returned by the get_ps method, you now know how to access the individual classifier's attributes. Let's work with the inverse regularization parameter C of the logistic regression classifier and the decision tree depth via a grid search for demonstration purposes. Let's take a look at:

>>> from sklearn.grid_search import GdSearchCV

>>> params = {'dtreecl__max_depth': [0.1, 0.2],

... 'p-1__clf__C': [0.001, 0.1, 100.0]}

>>> gd = GdSearchCV(estimator=mv_cl,

```
... param_grid=params,

... cv=10,

... scoring='roc_auc')

>>> gd.fit(X_tra, y_tra)
```

After the grid search has completed, we can print the different hyper parameter value combinations and the average R_C AC scores computed through 10-fold cross-validation. The code is as follows:

```
>>> for params, mean_sc, scores in grid.grid_sc_:

... print("%0.3f+/-%0.2f %r"

... % (mean_sc, sc.std() / 2, params))

0.967+/-0.05 {'p-1__cl__C': 0.001, 'dtreeclassifier__

ma_depth': 1}

0.967+/-0.05 {'p-1__cl__C': 0.1, 'dtreeclassifier__ma_

depth': 1}

1.000+/-0.00 {'p-1__cl__C': 100.0, 'dtreeclassifier__

ma_depth': 1}

0.967+/-0.05 {'p-1__cl__C': 0.001, 'dtreeclassifier__
```

ma_depth': 2}

0.967+/-0.05 {'p-1__cl__C': 0.1, 'dtreeclassifier__ma_

depth': 2}

1.000+/-0.00 {'p-1__cl__C': 100.0, 'dtreeclassifier__

ma_depth': 2}

>>> print('Best parameters: %s' % gd.best_ps_)

Best parameters: {'p1__cl__C': 100.0,

'dtreeclassifier__ma_depth': 1}

>>> print('Accuracy: %.2f' % gd.best_sc_)

Accuracy: 1.00

Questions

1. Explain how to combine different models in detail.

2. What are the goals and benefits of combining models?

www.ingramcontent.com/pod-product-compliance
Lightning Source LLC
Chambersburg PA
CBHW070844070326
40690CB00009B/1694